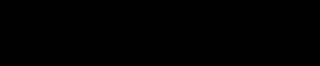

BOOK FIVE

Out Of The
Water

The most important event in the history of life on earth was the beginning of life. But the most important event *after that* was probably the movement of life out of the water and **onto the land.** Simple one-celled plants were probably the first living things on land. But it took a very long time for more complicated plants and animals to come out of the water— more than **3 billion years!** For all that time, the land looked as empty of life as the moon looks today. As you will see, there were some very good reasons why the land was so empty for so long . . .

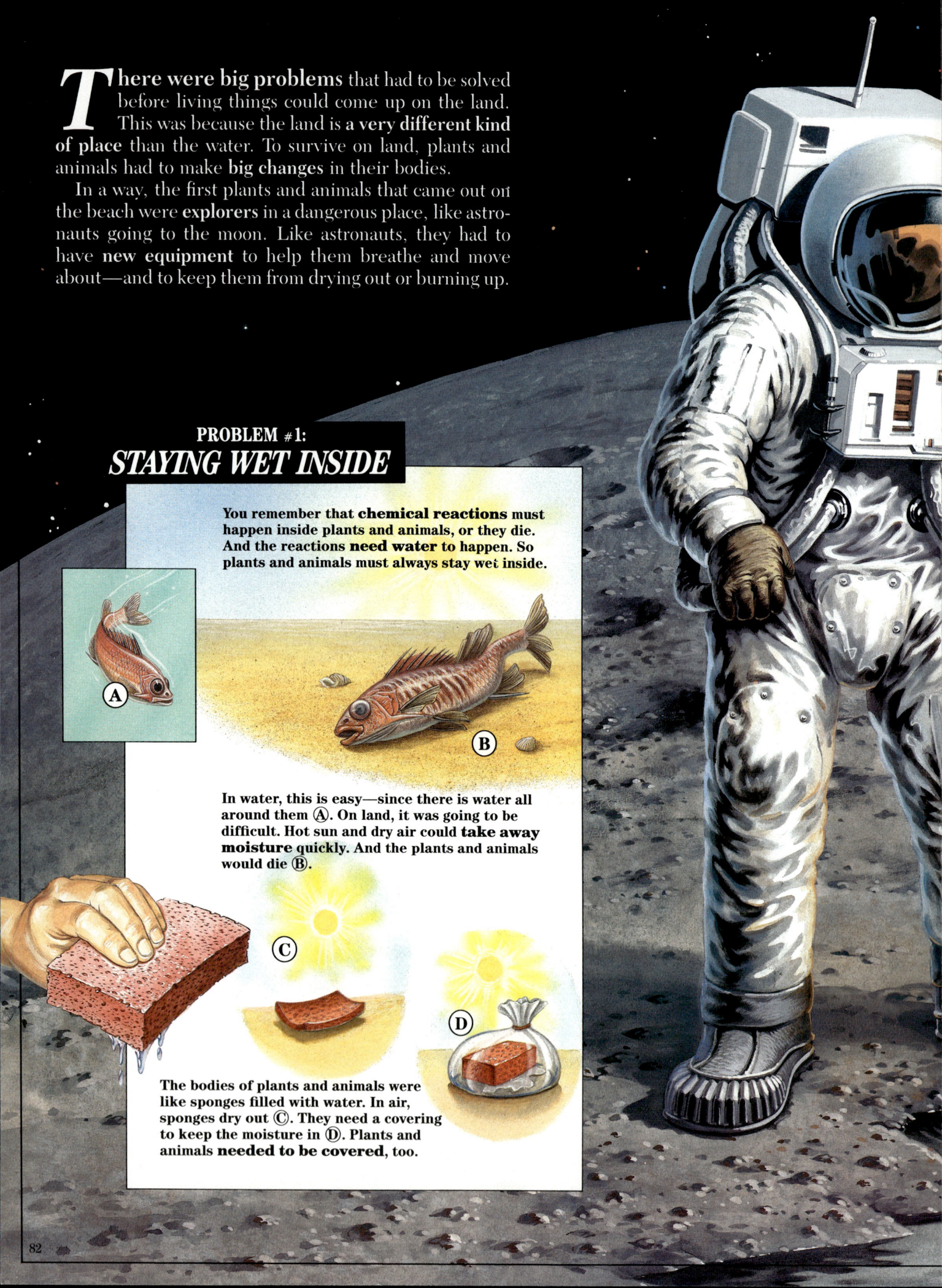

There were big problems that had to be solved before living things could come up on the land. This was because the land is a very different kind of place than the water. To survive on land, plants and animals had to make big changes in their bodies.

In a way, the first plants and animals that came out on the beach were explorers in a dangerous place, like astronauts going to the moon. Like astronauts, they had to have new equipment to help them breathe and move about—and to keep them from drying out or burning up.

PROBLEM #1: STAYING WET INSIDE

You remember that chemical reactions must happen inside plants and animals, or they die. And the reactions need water to happen. So plants and animals must always stay wet inside.

In water, this is easy—since there is water all around them Ⓐ. On land, it was going to be difficult. Hot sun and dry air could take away moisture quickly. And the plants and animals would die Ⓑ.

The bodies of plants and animals were like sponges filled with water. In air, sponges dry out Ⓒ. They need a covering to keep the moisture in Ⓓ. Plants and animals needed to be covered, too.

Out Of The *Water*

PREHISTORIC ZOOBOOKS

BOOK FIVE

Getting out of the water wasn't easy.

PROBLEM #2: BREATHING

1 Animals need oxygen to survive, and plants need carbon dioxide. In water, they could get these gases directly from the water. On land, they would have to get them **in other ways**.

2 You have already seen how fish developed **lungs** in shallow pools Ⓔ. These simple lungs allowed them to crawl to new pools if they needed to.

3 As time passed, they developed better lungs Ⓕ, and evolved into amphibians. These animals **could stay out of the water** for longer periods of time.

PROBLEM #3: STANDING UP

In water, it is easier for plants and animals to stand up—because **the water helps** to hold them up. On land, the force of gravity would pull them down. They would need **stronger skeletons** to help them stand up.

When you take a bath or go swimming, **you can see** how things weigh less in water. As you get out of the water, you can feel **how gravity pulls harder** on your body. Luckily, you have a strong skeleton inside your body to help you stand up and move about.

83

Plants were first to come up on the land. Simple one-celled plants probably left the water more than a billion years ago. But it took much longer for more complicated plants to develop ways to survive on land. **About 450 million years ago,** the first multi-celled plants were finally able to creep out on the shore.

There are very good reasons why plants came out before animals. The land was so empty that there was **nothing for animals to eat.** But there were minerals in the soil that plants could "eat." And there was water and sunlight to help them grow.

As you will see, the plants made it possible for animals to come out of the water—by providing food that animals could eat.

Some scientists believe that the first complicated plants on land evolved from complicated plants that lived in shallow pools of water. The pools were crowded with all kinds of living things—so the plants went up on the land to find more room to live.

Other scientists believe that complicated land plants Ⓐ evolved from simple one-celled plants Ⓑ that already lived on land. The simple plants are called **algae** (AL-gee).

For a long time, the plants **stayed close to the water**.

They adapted to life on land, and started to **spread out**.

After millions of years, they covered large areas of the land.

85

Plants were very successful on land. As you will see, they evolved some very good solutions to the problems of living on land. And they thrived.

After millions of years, there were **huge forests** of plants that covered most of the land. They were forests that would seem **very strange** to us. For one thing, most of the plants were **ferns and mosses**. There weren't any evergreen trees like firs, or broad-leafed trees like oaks and maples. And it was **very quiet**—because there weren't any birds or reptiles or mammals. For a long time, there weren't even any insects.

PROBLEM #1:
STAYING WET INSIDE

CUTICLE

WATER STAYS INSIDE

To keep moisture from escaping, plants "invented" a waxy coating called **a cuticle** (CUTE-uh-cul). Water was trapped inside the cuticle—but sunlight could pass through it for photosynthesis.

PROBLEM #2: BREATHING

Plants have millions of tiny "noses" on them.

CARBON DIOXIDE GOES IN

Ⓐ

Ⓑ

OXYGEN COMES OUT

When a plant "breathes," it takes in carbon dioxide gas and sends out oxygen. To do this, plants evolved special "noses" called **stomates** (STOW-mates). The stomates can open Ⓐ to let the gases go in or out—and then they close Ⓑ to keep water from getting out.

PROBLEM #3: STANDING UP

To help them stand up on land, many plants developed **tough woody fibers** in their bodies. The fibers were joined together to make stiff "skeletons," like the trunks and branches of trees. In this way, some plants were able **to grow tall** in spite of gravity.

TALLER PLANTS GET MORE SUNLIGHT.

The first animals on land probably came out of the water about 400 million years ago, looking for food. By that time, there were enough plants on the land to provide a lot of food. And plants had released enough oxygen into the air for small animals to breathe. So plant-eating animals could come out on the land **to eat the plants**.

The first land animals were probably small **arthropods** (ARE-thruh-podz), with hard armor on the outside and many legs—like the millipede shown below. As you will see, the bodies of arthropods didn't have to be changed too much to solve the problems of living on land.

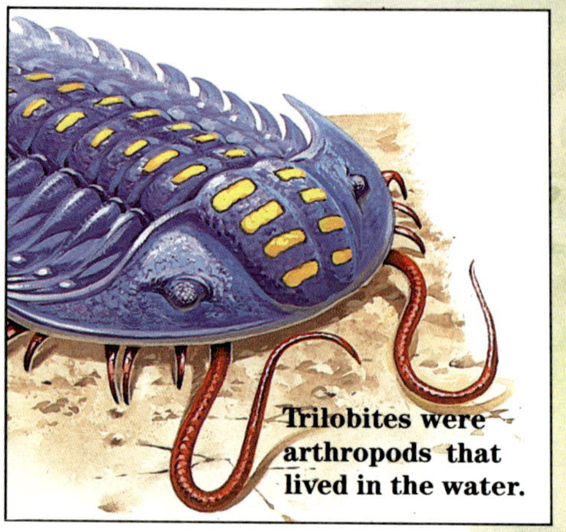

Trilobites were arthropods that lived in the water.

Arthropods lived in water for more than 200 million years before some of them came out on land. During that time, they evolved hard skeletons on **the outside** of their bodies. These were called **exoskeletons** (EX-O-skel-uh-tons), and they made it easier for arthropods to adapt to life on land.

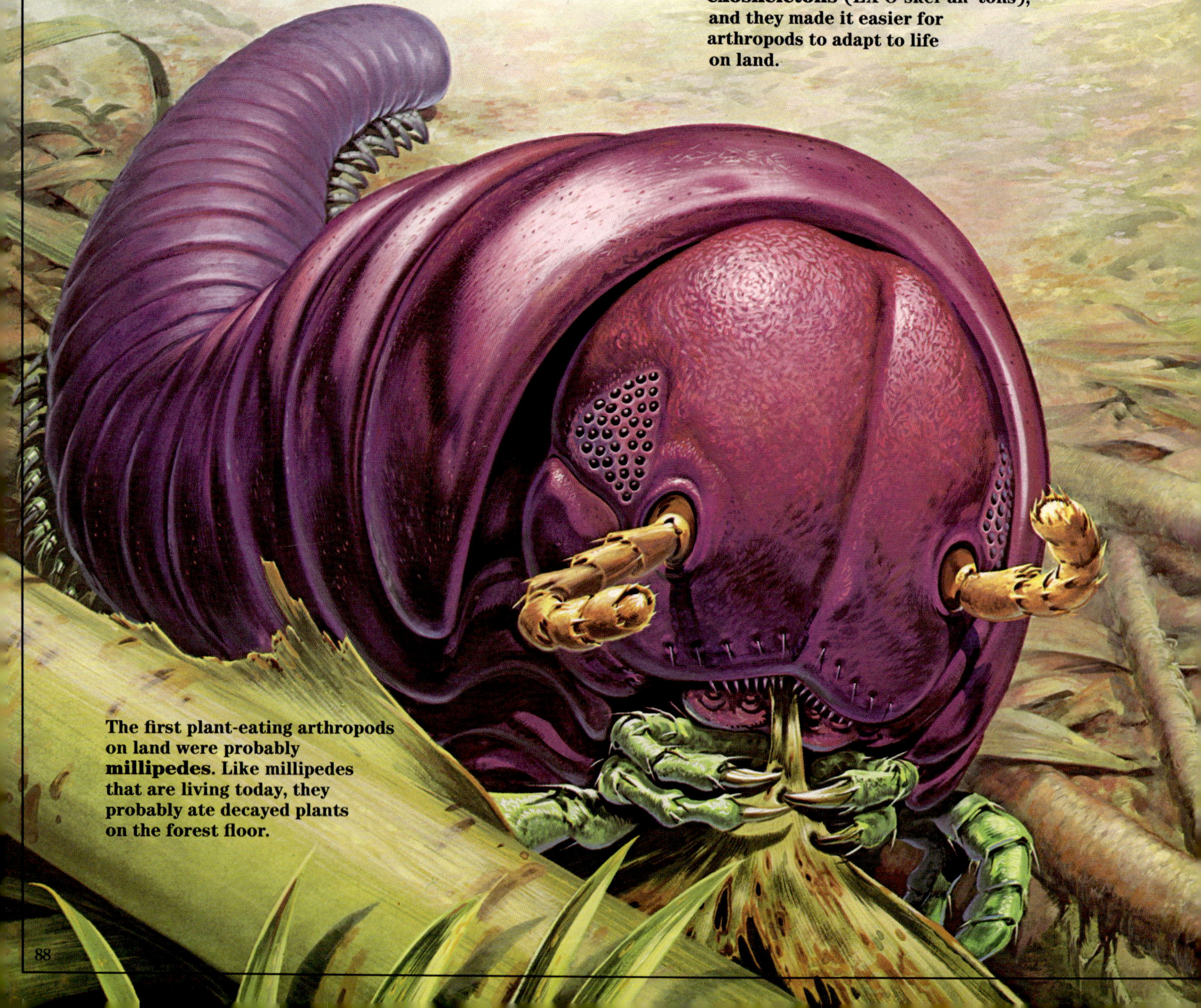

The first plant-eating arthropods on land were probably **millipedes**. Like millipedes that are living today, they probably ate decayed plants on the forest floor.

For a time, the land must have been a paradise for plant-eating arthropods. There was plenty of food, and no predators to eat them. But then, **meat-eating arthropods** came out of the water and started to eat the plant-eaters. The first meat-eaters on land were probably **scorpions**.

PROBLEM #1: *STAYING WET INSIDE*

In water, exoskeletons protected arthropods from predators. On land, they also helped **to keep the water inside** their bodies. The hard layers of the exoskeleton Ⓐ were made of a very hard material called **chitin** (KY-tin). Like glass, the chitin kept moisture from getting out Ⓑ.

PROBLEM #3: *STANDING UP*

The exoskeleton on arthropods was **already very stiff** in the water. On land, it could provide plenty of support Ⓓ to hold up the body against the pull of gravity.

PROBLEM #2: *BREATHING*

In water, arthropods breathed through gills. On land, the gills evolved into simple **"breathing tubes."** Like plants, the arthropods had holes Ⓒ in their hard outer covering—to let gases in and out as they breathed. The holes could be closed to keep moisture from escaping.

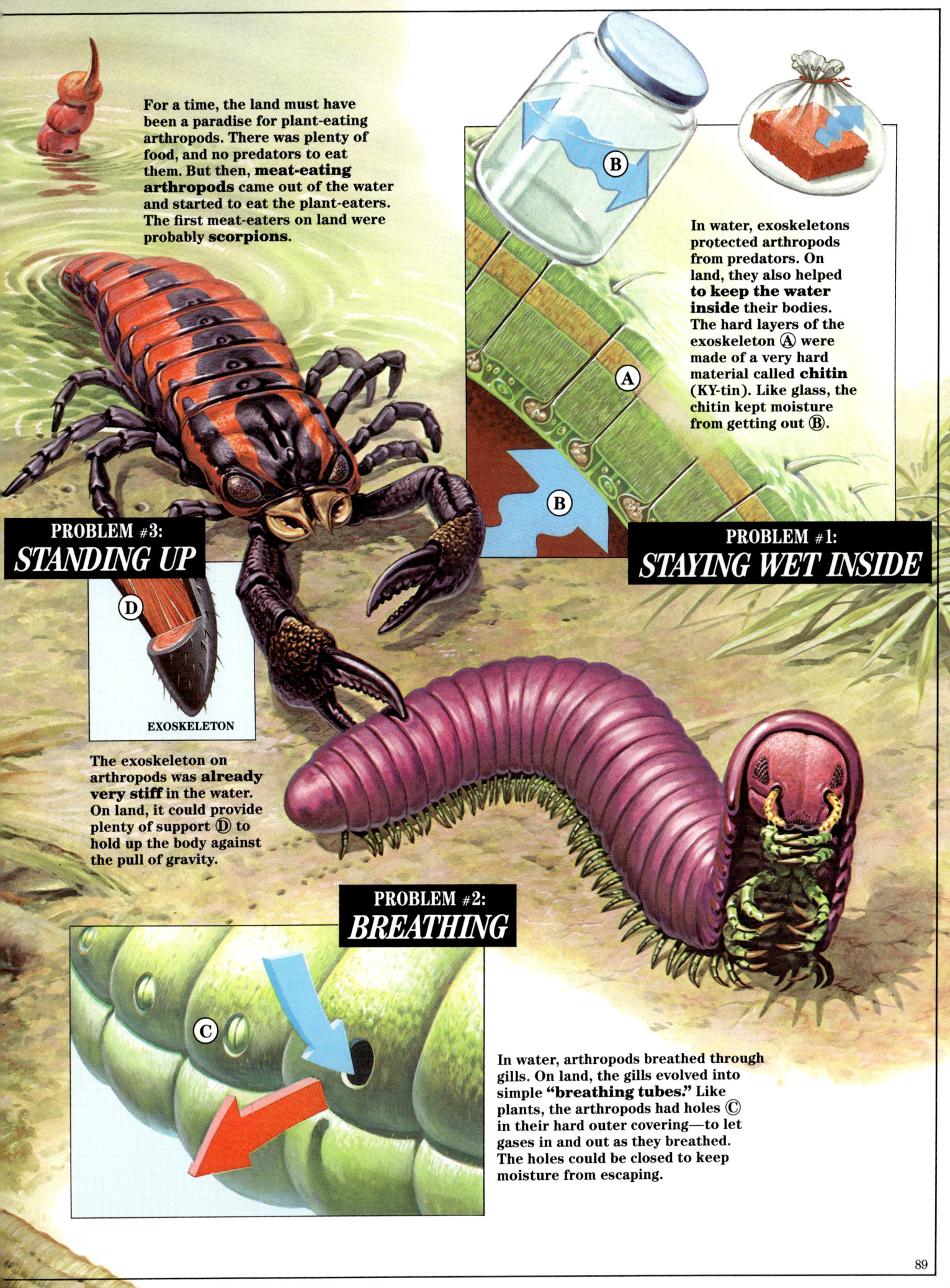

The most successful group of arthropods on land was (and still *is*) the insects. They started to evolve soon after the first arthropods came out of the water—and before long, there were many types of insects *all over the place!*

There were several reasons why insects were so successful. They were very good at getting food. They could reproduce themselves in large numbers. And perhaps most important of all— *many of them could fly.* Insects were **the first animals on earth to have wings.**

Wings were a wonderful "invention"—and for a long time, insects were the only animals that had them. They could use their wings **to escape** from predators. They could use them to fly to new places **to find food**—places that other animals could not reach. No wonder that insects were so successful!

There were plant-eating insects and meat-eating insects. Some of the meat-eaters grew **very large**— much larger than the insects we know today. There were dragonflies with wings that were **more than two feet long!**

THE FIRST WINGS

Early insects had **no wings** Ⓐ. But some of them were born with **small flaps** on their sides Ⓑ. Over millions of years, the flaps evolved into **wings.**

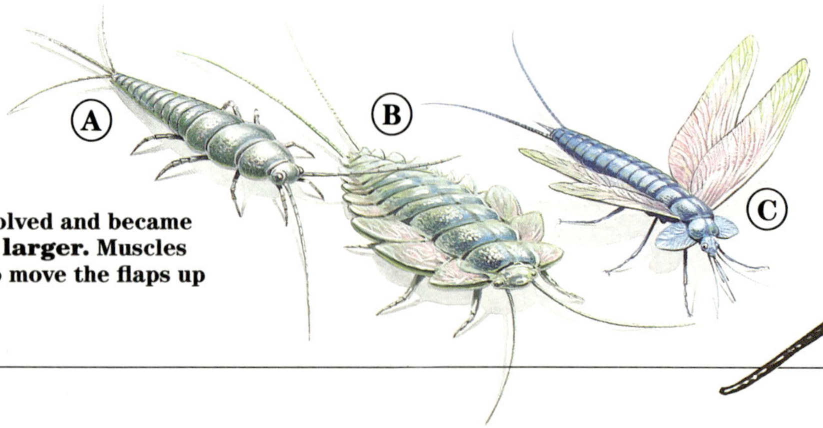

The flaps evolved and became **larger and larger.** Muscles developed to move the flaps up and down.

After a long time, the flaps finally evolved into **two sets of wings** Ⓒ—one pair in front and one in back.

90

FOLDING WINGS

Big wings are wonderful for flying up in the air. But on the ground, they can make it hard for an insect to move around. this is why beetles and other insects developed wings that can be **folded out of the way**.

The front wings of beetles evolved into **hard covers** G. The back wings could be folded *under the covers* H. This made it easy for beetles to **burrow into the ground** I without harming their wings.

Beetles combine the advantages of flying insects and ground insects. They can fly in the air to find food and escape predators. *And* they can burrow in the ground to find food and escape predators.

Many insects today start their lives as caterpillars, **without wings** D. Their bodies change inside a cocoon E and they come out of the cocoon **with wings** F.

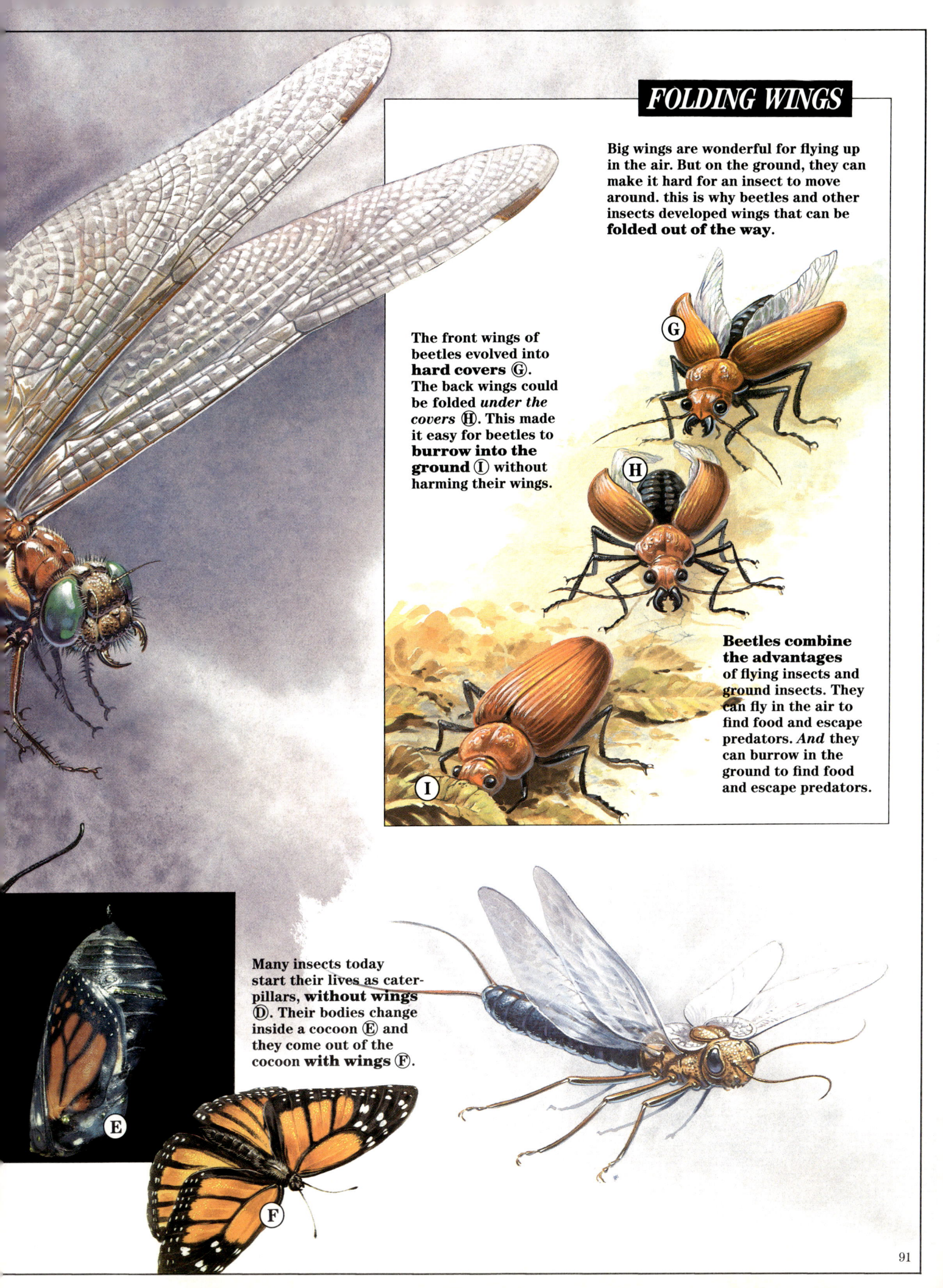

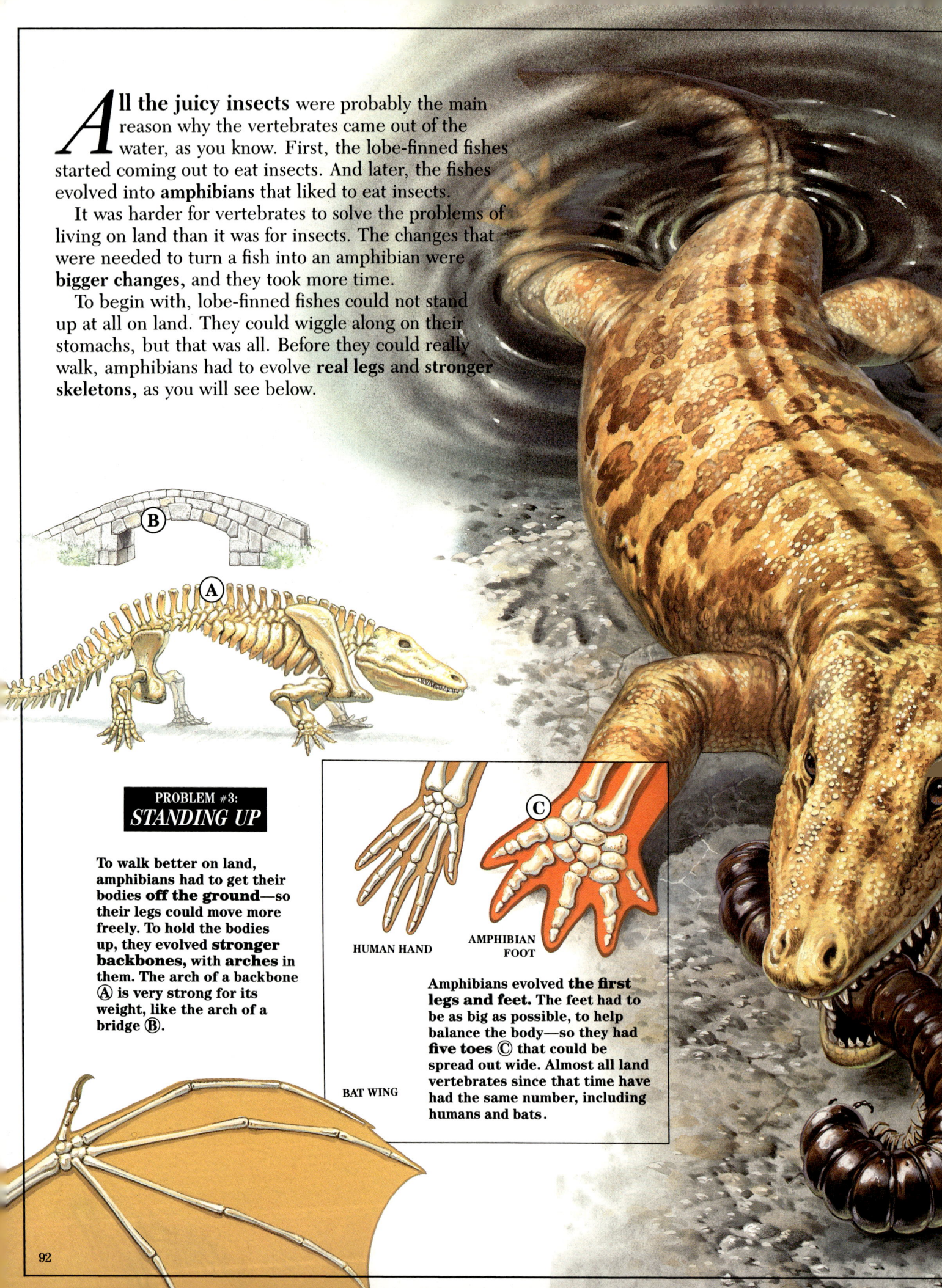

All the juicy insects were probably the main reason why the vertebrates came out of the water, as you know. First, the lobe-finned fishes started coming out to eat insects. And later, the fishes evolved into **amphibians** that liked to eat insects.

It was harder for vertebrates to solve the problems of living on land than it was for insects. The changes that were needed to turn a fish into an amphibian were **bigger changes,** and they took more time.

To begin with, lobe-finned fishes could not stand up at all on land. They could wiggle along on their stomachs, but that was all. Before they could really walk, amphibians had to evolve **real legs** and **stronger skeletons,** as you will see below.

PROBLEM #3: STANDING UP

To walk better on land, amphibians had to get their bodies **off the ground**—so their legs could move more freely. To hold the bodies up, they evolved **stronger backbones,** with **arches** in them. The arch of a backbone Ⓐ is very strong for its weight, like the arch of a bridge Ⓑ.

Amphibians evolved **the first legs and feet.** The feet had to be as big as possible, to help balance the body—so they had **five toes** Ⓒ that could be spread out wide. Almost all land vertebrates since that time have had the same number, including humans and bats.

HUMAN HAND

AMPHIBIAN FOOT

BAT WING

PROBLEM #2: BREATHING

As you know, lobe-finned fishes had lungs Ⓓ. These evolved into **larger and stronger lungs** Ⓔ—so amphibians could breathe air better, and stay out of the water longer than the fishes.

HEARING ON LAND

Good hearing was necessary for amphibians, so they could hear prey coming—or hear animals coming that might want to eat them. The problem was, **sound travels differently** on land than it does in water. So the method that fish used to hear in water could not be used on land. It had to be changed—and the way this happened should interest you very much . . . because it determined **the way that your ears work!**

FISH "EAR"

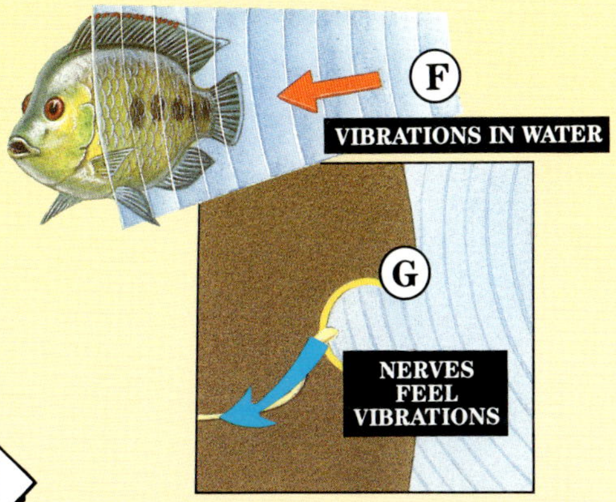

Ⓕ VIBRATIONS IN WATER

Ⓖ NERVES FEEL VIBRATIONS

① IN WATER, when something makes a sound **the water moves** Ⓕ. The movements are called **vibrations** (vy-BRAY-shuns). Fish have special holes on the sides of their bodies Ⓖ with nerves in them—and these nerves **can feel vibrations in water**. When they feel vibrations, the fish "hear".

AMPHIBIAN EAR

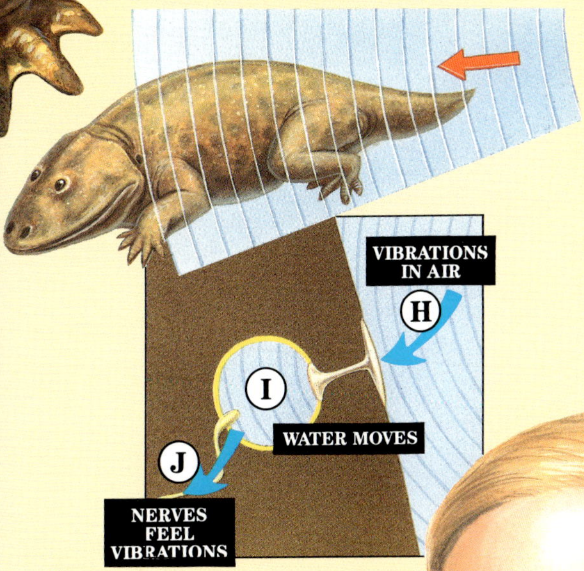

VIBRATIONS IN AIR Ⓗ

Ⓘ WATER MOVES

Ⓙ NERVES FEEL VIBRATIONS

HUMAN EAR

WATER MOVES

NERVES FEEL VIBRATIONS

VIBRATIONS IN AIR

② ON LAND, sounds make vibrations **in the air**. So amphibians had to adapt the fish system of hearing so it could feel these different vibrations. Amphibians have **pools of water inside their heads** Ⓗ. Sound from the air comes into their ears and stirs up the water Ⓘ. Nerves **feel the water moving** Ⓙ and the amphibian hears.

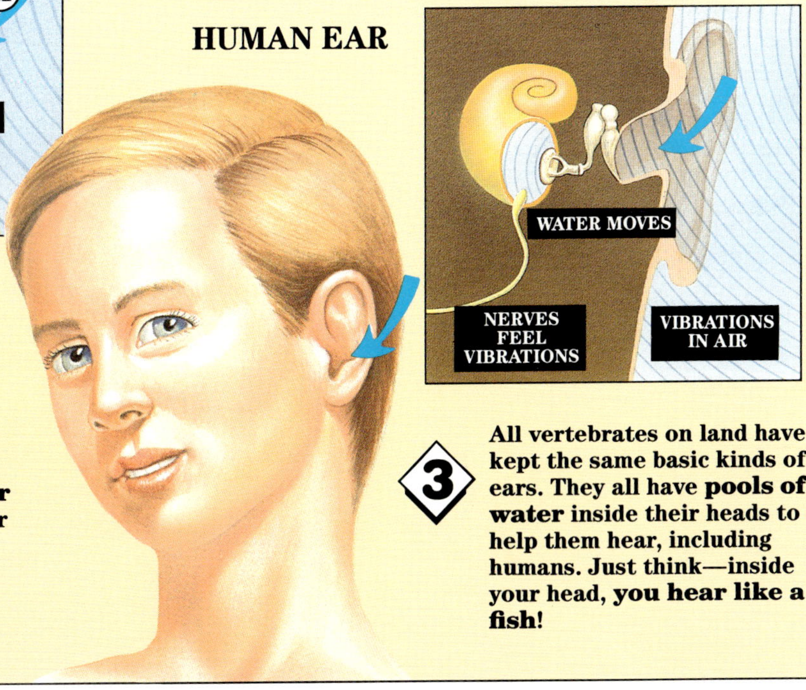

③ All vertebrates on land have kept the same basic kinds of ears. They all have **pools of water** inside their heads to help them hear, including humans. Just think—inside your head, **you hear like a fish!**

93

PROBLEM #1: STAYING WET INSIDE

Amphibians need to stay near water to stay alive. When they evolved from fish, they never developed a good way to keep their bodies **wet inside** on land. They can stay out of water longer than a fish—but if they stay out **too long**, they will dry out and die. This is why all amphibians live **in moist places**.

Amphibians also need water **to have babies**. Like fish most amphibians lay their eggs in water. Their babies look like fish for the first part of their lives—and only later do they develop legs for use on land. Amphibians are really only **partly land animals**.

Amphibians have never been able to solve this problem completely. Their skins cannot hold moisture inside their bodies very well—so they **must keep their skins moist** to keep their bodies from drying out. This means that all amphibians **must live in moist places** like swamps, where they can get wet when they need to.

DANGEROUS FOR BABIES

1 Most amphibians go back into the water to lay their eggs. There are many predators in the water that like to eat eggs —so amphibians have to lay **lots of eggs**.

2 Even if they hatch, the young are **still in danger**. There are plenty of predators that like to eat young amphibians.

Amphibians could not survive outside moist areas. So they could only live on **part of the land**.

Outside of the moist areas, there were large areas of land that were **too dry** for amphibians. They would never be able to live in such places.

To help more of their babies survive, some types of amphibians "invented" a way to **lay eggs on land**.

Amphibian eggs that are laid on land must still be **kept moist**. So they are usually laid on wet ground and covered with moist soil and leaves. Inside the eggs, the baby amphibians develop **as they would in water**. First, they have tails like fish. And then they grow legs. When they hatch, they are ready to live on land—**part of the time**.

③ **If they live long enough**, baby amphibians finally develop legs—and they can move out of the water. Only a few of them make it. Out of the thousands of eggs that are laid by an amphibian **only a handful** survive to grow up.

REMEMBER:

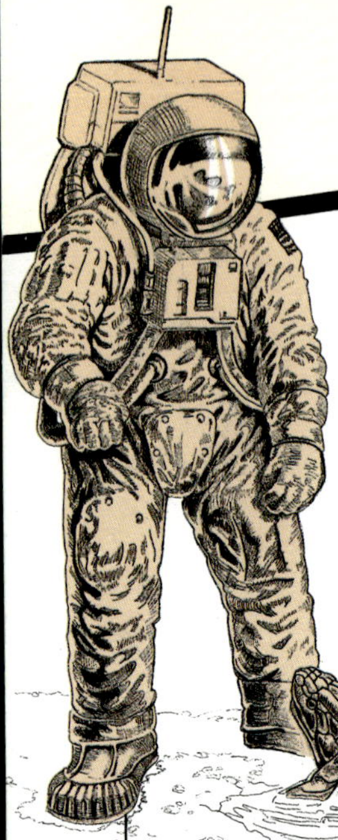

1 It took **a long time** for the first plants and animals to come out of the water—more than 3 billion years. Like astronauts, plants and animals had to develop **new equipment** to help them survive in a dangerous place.

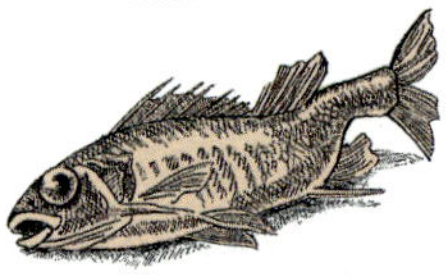

2 They had to develop ways to keep their bodies **wet inside.**

3 They had to evolve ways **to breathe** out of the water.

4 And they needed skeletons that could **hold their bodies up** on land.

5 **Plants were the first** to come out of the water. They developed **cuticles** to keep their bodies wet inside.

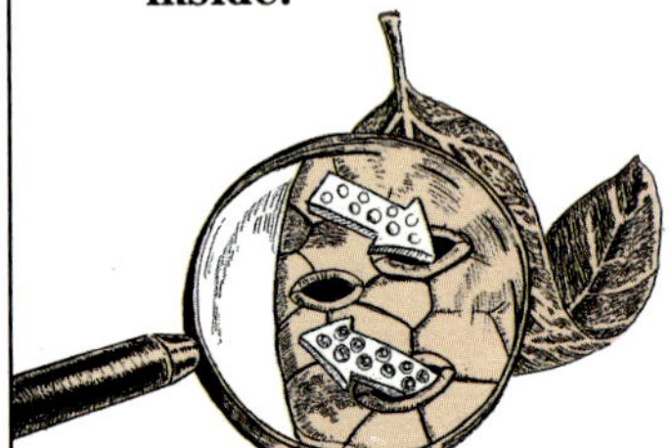

6 To breathe, plants evolved **stomates** that could open to let carbon dioxide in and oxygen out.

7 Many plants developed skeletons of **tough woody fibers** to help them stand up.

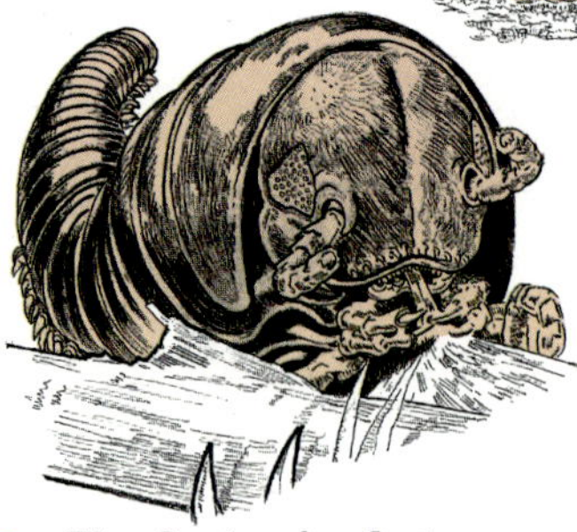

8 The first animals to come out of the water were **arthropods.** They came out to eat plants.

9 In water, arthropods had tough shells on the outside of their bodies called **exoskeletons.** On land, these shells helped them to **keep moisture inside** their bodies.

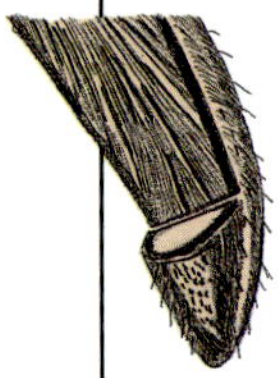

10 The exoskeletons of arthropods were strong enough **to hold their bodies up** on land, so they could move around.

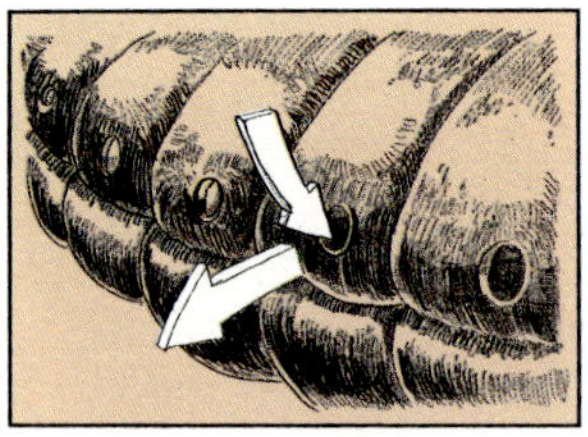

11 To breathe on land, arthropods developed special **breathing tubes.**

12 The most successful group of arthropods on land are **the insects.** Insects were **the first animals to fly,** and this was one big reason for their success.

NEW WORDS:

Algae
(Al-gee):
Simple one-celled plants. The first plants on land were probably algae.

Cuticle
(CUTE-uh-cul):
The hard outer covering of a plant that helps to keep moisture in.

Stomate:
(STOW-mate):
Opening in the cuticle that lets the plant "breathe." It lets carbon dioxide in and oxygen out.

13 Fish were the first vertebrates to come out of the water. They probably came out **to eat insects**. Over millions of years, the fish evolved into **amphibians.**

14 The fish had simple lungs to breathe out of the water. Amphibians evolved **better lungs** to breathe better.

15 To stand up on land, amphibians evolved skeletons with **real legs** and **stronger backbones.**

16 Amphibians evolved **the first feet** to help them stand up better. There were **five toes** on each foot—and many vertebrates still have the same number.

17 Amphibians need to stay **close to water**. They can only live in wet places, like swamps.

18 Most amphibians lay their eggs in water. But the water is **a dangerous place** for young amphibians.

19 To help more babies survive, some types of amphibians started to **lay eggs on land.**

Arthropods
(ARE-thruh-podz):
Group of hard-shelled animals. The first land animals were probably arthropods.

Exoskeleton
(EX-o-skel-uh-tun):
Hard outer shell of an arthropod.

Chitin
(KY-tin):
The material that exoskeletons are made of.

Vibrations
(vy-BRAY-shuns):
Movements in water or air caused by sound. Hearing depends on vibrations.

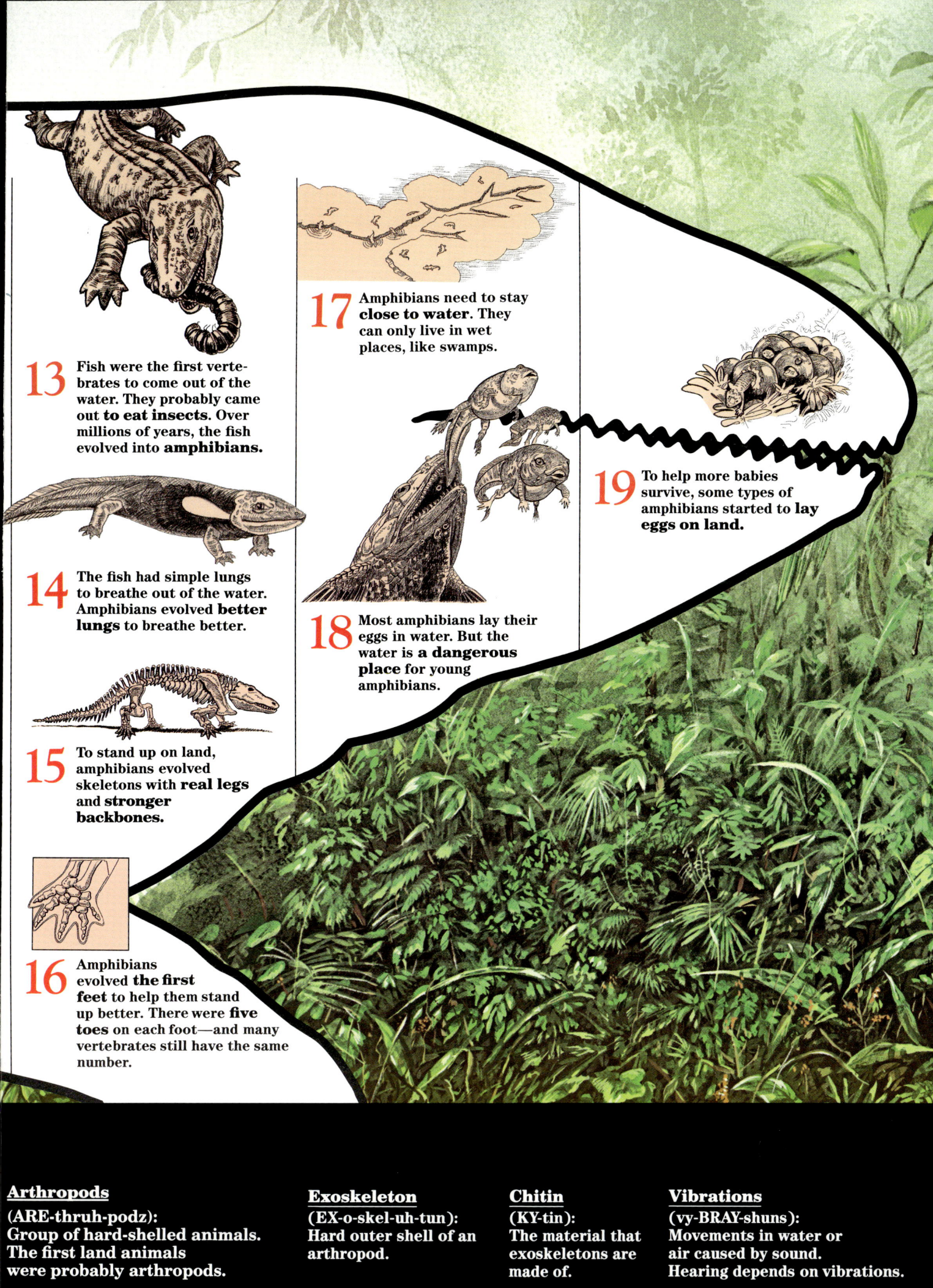

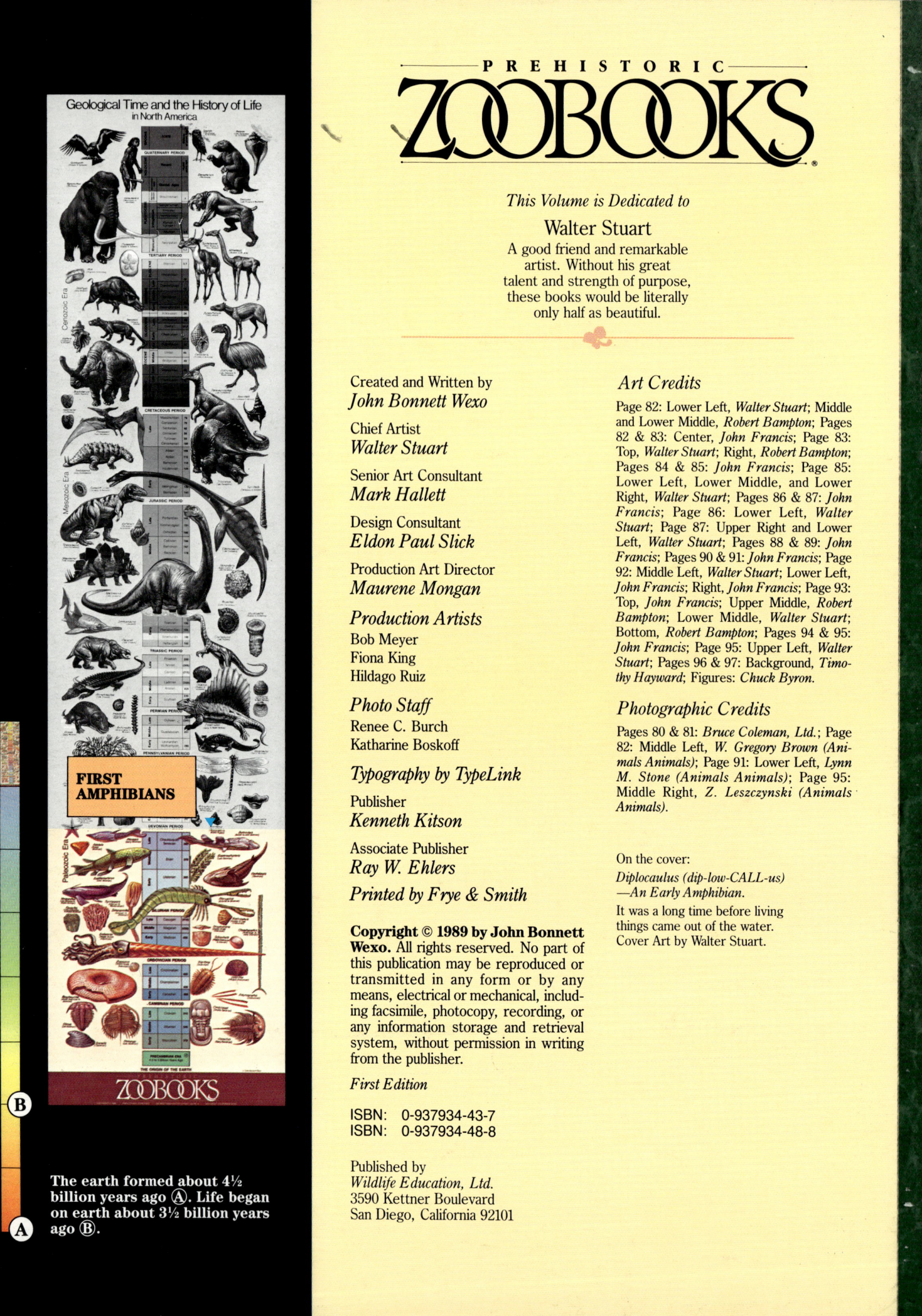

Geological Time and the History of Life in North America

FIRST AMPHIBIANS

The earth formed about 4½ billion years ago Ⓐ. Life began on earth about 3½ billion years ago Ⓑ.

PREHISTORIC ZOOBOOKS

This Volume is Dedicated to

Walter Stuart

A good friend and remarkable artist. Without his great talent and strength of purpose, these books would be literally only half as beautiful.

Created and Written by
John Bonnett Wexo

Chief Artist
Walter Stuart

Senior Art Consultant
Mark Hallett

Design Consultant
Eldon Paul Slick

Production Art Director
Maurene Mongan

Production Artists
Bob Meyer
Fiona King
Hildago Ruiz

Photo Staff
Renee C. Burch
Katharine Boskoff

Typography by TypeLink

Publisher
Kenneth Kitson

Associate Publisher
Ray W. Ehlers

Printed by Frye & Smith

Copyright © 1989 by John Bonnett Wexo. All rights reserved. No part of this publication may be reproduced or transmitted in any form or by any means, electrical or mechanical, including facsimile, photocopy, recording, or any information storage and retrieval system, without permission in writing from the publisher.

First Edition

ISBN: 0-937934-43-7
ISBN: 0-937934-48-8

Published by
Wildlife Education, Ltd.
3590 Kettner Boulevard
San Diego, California 92101

Art Credits

Page 82: Lower Left, *Walter Stuart*; Middle and Lower Middle, *Robert Bampton*; Pages 82 & 83: Center, *John Francis*; Page 83: Top, *Walter Stuart*; Right, *Robert Bampton*; Pages 84 & 85: *John Francis*; Page 85: Lower Left, Lower Middle, and Lower Right, *Walter Stuart*; Pages 86 & 87: *John Francis*; Page 86: Lower Left, *Walter Stuart*; Page 87: Upper Right and Lower Left, *Walter Stuart*; Pages 88 & 89: *John Francis*; Pages 90 & 91: *John Francis*; Page 92: Middle Left, *Walter Stuart*; Lower Left, *John Francis*; Right, *John Francis*; Page 93: Top, *John Francis*; Upper Middle, *Robert Bampton*; Lower Middle, *Walter Stuart*; Bottom, *Robert Bampton*; Pages 94 & 95: *John Francis*; Page 95: Upper Left, *Walter Stuart*; Pages 96 & 97: Background, *Timothy Hayward*; Figures: *Chuck Byron*.

Photographic Credits

Pages 80 & 81: *Bruce Coleman, Ltd.*; Page 82: Middle Left, *W. Gregory Brown (Animals Animals)*; Page 91: Lower Left, *Lynn M. Stone (Animals Animals)*; Page 95: Middle Right, *Z. Leszczynski (Animals Animals)*.

On the cover:
Diplocaulus (dip-low-CALL-us)
—An Early Amphibian.
It was a long time before living things came out of the water.
Cover Art by Walter Stuart.